MOTIVATION THEORY FOR TEACHERS

A Programed Book

MADELINE HUNTER, ED.D
Principal, University Elementary School
Lecturer, Graduate School of Education
University of California, Los Angeles
Educational Consultant

TIP PUBLICATIONS
El Segundo, California

THEORY INTO PRACTICE PUBLICATIONS

Motivation Theory for Teachers

Reinforcement Theory for Teachers

Retention Theory for Teachers

Teach More—Faster!

Teach for Transfer

Additional Publications

Aide-ing in Education

Prescription For Improved Instruction

Improving Your Child's Behavior

Parent-Teacher Conferencing

Mastery Teaching

Copyright © 1967, by Madeline Hunter
TIP Publications P.O. Box 514
El Segundo, California 90245

Thirty-Second Printing, December, 1984
Thirty-Third Printing, April, 1985
Thirty-Fourth Printing, July, 1985
Thirty-Fifth Printing, August, 1985
Thirty-Sixth Printing, October, 1985
Thirty-Seventh Printing, June, 1986
Thirty-Eighth Printing, January, 1987

ISBN 0-935567-00-3

PRINTED IN THE UNITED STATES OF AMERICA

FOREWORD

Psychological knowledge that will result in significantly increased learning of students is now available for teachers. In most cases, this knowledge remains unused because it is written in language that takes an advanced statistician to decode, or is buried in research journals in university libraries.

This book is one of a series written to make this important knowledge available to the classroom teacher. As such it makes no attempt to achieve comprehensive coverage of the subject, but endeavors to interpret that knowledge which is most useful in the daily decisions of teachers. The purist in learning theory may complain that some generalizations are over-simplified. Our answer would be that understanding a theory in simple form is necessary to the desire to search for increasing ramifications and complexities. The reader must also be warned that decisions based on learning theory are decisions of HOW to teach. These decisions can be made only AFTER the teacher has made decisions of WHAT content to teach and WHICH objectives are appropriate for the learner in that content area.

In other words, once a teacher has identified an appropriate educational destination for the learner, knowledge of learning theory will reveal the most effective, efficient and economical route to reach that destination.

Appreciation is expressed to the professors who made psychological theory meaningful to me when I was a student, to Dr. May Seagoe who encouraged me with her belief that it is important for all teachers, to Mrs. Margaret Devers and Mrs. Elsa Gilbert whose ability to decode my writing made a manuscript possible, and to the many teachers I have trained who continually reaffirmed my belief that there is nothing more practical than a valid theory.

Madeline Hunter

To my family who survived it, this
book is affectionately dedicated.

MOTIVATION THEORY FOR TEACHERS

"How do I make Johnny learn?" is the question that has plagued all teachers since the beginning of time. The answer is simple. It can't be done! No one can *make* a child or anyone else learn. At best, circumstances in the environment can be arranged so a child will be encouraged to do something that will result in his learning.

There are some things we can't do anything about such as a child's family, his physical structure, how many brothers or sisters he has. There are other things we can change or vary in the environment. We call these "variables" that are subject to our control. The assignment in the book, the way we talk to a child, where he sits, or the amount and kind of work he has to do are all "variables" we can change. With a certain goal in mind, we say we are manipulating these variables when we change them in order to reach that goal.

Let's see how clear this is. Paul is a boy who has a great deal of difficulty keeping his hands to himself when he is walking with a group. The teacher, knowing this, asks him if he will assist her by carrying a stack of books. With his hands loaded, Paul is able to walk with the group to the library without any trouble.

What variable of the task of walking to the library was the teacher manipulating? Choose the answer you think is right and turn to the page indicated.

a. the interest of the task . . . turn to the top of page 2.
b. the feeling tone of the task . . . turn to the bottom of page 2.
c. the reward of the task . . . turn to the top of page 3.
d. the difficulty of the task . . . turn to the bottom of page 3.

a. **You said the teacher was manipulating the variable of the interest of the task.**

Possibly. If the books are heavy enough, Paul may have a real interest in getting to a place where he can dump them. However, it was his hands being occupied that kept them out of trouble. Turn back to the question on page 1 and choose an answer that shows the teacher manipulated a variable that increased Paul's chance for walking successfully.

b. **You said the teacher was manipulating the variable of the feeling tone of the task.**

Possibly. If Paul likes the teacher, he'll enjoy helping her. If he doesn't like her, he'll wish she'd carry her own books. However, it was his hands being occupied that kept him out of trouble, not the feeling tone of the task. Turn back to the question on page 1 and choose an answer that shows the teacher was manipulating a variable that increased Paul's chance for success.

c. You said the teacher had manipulated the variable of the reward of the task.

The only reward involved might be the teacher's approval or his own feeling of success. Granted, that's mighty important; but you need to turn back to the question on page 1 and choose an answer that shows what variable the teacher manipulated to be sure he would be successful.

d. You said the teacher had manipulated the variable of the difficulty of the task.

Right you are! It's a lot easier to take care of your hands if they're already occupied, than if they're free and available for any activity that might interest or tempt them. By occupying his hands, the teacher made it *easier* for Paul to walk successfully to the library. The problem of his hands is far from solved, but now that he has had a successful experience he should be motivated to try to do it again. The teacher can start increasing the difficulty of the task by having him walk a little way with his hands free and then giving him something to carry. This is just like gradually increasing the difficulty of the book in reading, the problems in arithmetic, or the pounds in weight lifting. You are manipulating the variable of the difficulty of the task to increase motivation.

Now turn to the next page . . .

Now that you understand what we mean when we say we are manipulating variables, let's look at how this knowledge will help us if we wish motivation to increase. Please remember, the purpose of this program is to teach you about motivation. It is not a book of what-a-teacher-should-do recipes.

We need to begin by defining motivation as a *state of need or desire that activates the person to do something that will satisfy that need or desire.* It is important to realize that motivation is a state of unresolved need or desire existing *within* the child. Therefore, we cannot "motivate" him. We can manipulate environmental variables that *may* result in an increase or decrease of motivation (inner state of need or desire).

As an example, hunger is a state of desire or need that exists in most school boys. We can't make a boy hungry. By keeping him in at noon to finish his work, we are manipulating (withholding) the environmental variable (food) that should result in increased need (hunger). Therefore, he may be activated to finish his work so he can eat and resolve his inner need (he won't be hungry any more).

Food, rest, air, and physical comfort are all obvious needs. Security, safety, feeling of belonging, individual worth, and stimulation by the environment are less obvious needs, but they are important to us as we teach. Occasionally, we may work with a need such as hunger in the example cited, but most of the time at school we deal with motivation resulting from needs such as feelings of worth and security.

We all have experienced the frustration of the "unmotivated student" who passively resists the pressure of his parents, the societal expectations for learning, and the brilliance of our teaching —

What can we do?

a. we can *make* him learn . . . turn to page 5, top.
b. we can give up and devote our efforts to motivated students . . . turn to page 5, bottom.
c. we can manipulate some variable that we predict will result in his becoming more motivated to learn . . . turn to page 6, top.
d. we can wait until he becomes motivated . . . turn to page 6, bottom.

4

a. **You said we can *make* him learn.**

   It can't be done! You could load a gun and threaten to shoot him if he doesn't learn, but he might prefer to die. Turn back to the question on page 4. All the other answers *can* be done. Choose the one that indicates professional know-how.

b. **You said we can give up and devote our efforts to motivated students.**

   A lot of teachers have done just that. However, motivated students can learn from books, programs, and television so you may surplus yourself. Besides, you'll have trouble with your own feelings of guilt and frustration as you ignore the reluctant learner. Turn back to the question on page 4 and choose an answer that indicates a teacher is indispensable to the unmotivated student.

c. You said we can manipulate some variable that we predict will
result in his becoming more motivated to learn.

You bet we can! That kind of decision shows professional know-
how. It's easier than you think. Research has identified several
factors that are related to motivation. Your motivation to find out
what they are and some ways to use them should result in your
turning to the next page.

d. You said we can wait until he becomes motivated.

That may be when we're in our wheel chairs, or never! Besides,
there is no point in our being a teacher if that's what we plan to
do. Turn back to the question on page 4 and choose an answer
to the question that shows our professional know-how will be used.

Two of the variables that are related to motivation are concerned with the learner's feelings. They are 1) the degree of concern or tension that exists within the learner and 2) the feeling tone, i.e., whether it's pleasant, unpleasant or neutral.

Other variables known to be related to the amount of motivation are the degree of 1) interest, 2) success, 3) difficulty, 4) knowledge of results, and 5) relation of the activity to an internalized goal. As with all human behavior, no one factor exists in complete independence; all are interrelated. We separate them for the purpose of learning about them, but we work with many variables at one time, concentrating on those that are most responsive to our environmental manipulation.

Let's take each of these variables and see how we might manipulate it to increase motivation. On some occasions, you may find that factors related to motivation are producing so much tension that you wish to reduce their influence. In this case, you will need to reverse the process that you ordinarily follow to increase motivation.

1. Degree of Concern or Tension

Most of us feel that anxiety or tension is undesirable. However, a certain amount of tension or concern is essential to motivation. If everything is just right, you are motivated to do only what's necessary to keep it that way. Picture yourself after a good day and a good dinner in a soft chair in a comfortable room with nothing that must be done. What are you motivated to do? Very little!

Now suppose in your contented state you receive a phone call and are informed you are to have read the contents of this program on motivation by tomorrow morning. You may not do anything about it, but you are no longer in your state of equilibrium. To resolve your restless state you may decide to read the program and get it over with, or to read it later in the evening, or to read it in the morning, or to ignore it and "hang the consequences."

Now suppose the phone rings again and you are told you will be tested on the content of this program. Your concern or tension will probably increase. You may decide to get at the task, or you may stick with your previous decision.

Now suppose you get a third call telling you that the results of the test will be posted for all your fellow teachers to see. You might still enjoy the evening and not read this (adjective deleted) program until tomorrow morning, but the chances are that your concern or anxiety has increased to a point where you are no longer comfortable so you might just as well get at the task.

Suppose you now learn that the superintendent's decision about your employment will be based on whether you receive a perfect score on the motivation test. Our bet is that you are all through resting and relaxing and this program is in your hot hands. By this time, your tension has turned into either anger or anxiety, and a great deal of the energy you might be directing to reading is being used to deal with your emotions. It's hard to keep your mind on this program (you have added several other adjectives that need deleting). Your mind keeps wandering to the unfairness of the situation, the unreasonableness of the superintendent, and to your need to reassure yourself that there is no reason you can't learn the confounded material and get a perfect score.

In considering our hypothetical situation we have developed the important generalization about tension that should guide our teaching decisions. No tension or concern—no motivation. Tension increases motivation up to a point. Beyond that point the learner must use some of his energy to handle his tension. Consequently, he does not have as much energy to devote to the learning task.

Let's practice applying this principle to a classroom situation

Adolescent Sally sits inertly over her math assignment. She is majoring in boys, and is perfectly contented to ignore the trivia of a math paper. We decide to manipulate her environment so we can build some tension. Which action will probably be most effective?

a. ignoring the situation so she's not embarrassed . . . turn to page 10, top.
b. reminding her she has a math paper due . . . turn to page 10, bottom.
c. telling her she will miss her recess if her work is not completed . . . turn to page 11, top.
d. telling her she will be sent to a younger group if she can't work . . . turn to page 11, bottom.

a. You said to ignore the situation so she's not embarrassed.

That will make it unanimous, because she's certainly ignoring it. She is not concerned or she wouldn't just be sitting there doing nothing. You need to jar her out of it. Turn back to page 9 and choose an answer that will build the most productive amount of tension.

b. You said to remind her that she has a math paper due.

It might help, but we doubt it. Usually children like this have learned not to let "reminders" upset their passive state. Turn back to the question on page 9 and choose the answer that will generate more tension.

c. **You said to tell her she will miss recess if her work is not completed.**

Good for you! You are making it clear that you are not going to accept an unfinished paper. Also, if she's interested in boys she's going to miss some golden opportunities at recess. Your strategy may not always work, but you are using learning principles correctly. That is the purpose of this program rather than developing a what-to-do-about-unfinished-work recipe.
Turn to page 12 to learn more about tension.

d. **You said to tell her she will be sent to a younger group if she can't work.**

You are building tension all right, and younger boys are not so fascinating but a lot of her energy will be directed to thinking about how mean you are, how much she hates math, and that she can't wait until she gets out of school. I think you will agree that none of these thoughts is likely to be facilitating to computation.
Turn back to page 9 and select an answer that will build some tension without such undesirable side effects.

It is not unusual for a child to come to us with too much anxiety. In this case our decision to manipulate the environment to *de*crease tension should produce *in*creased motivation.

Johnny's mother is impossible to live with if he doesn't bring home a perfect spelling test each Friday. He practices spelling all week, but works himself into such a frenzy by Friday that his test is a jumble of transposed letters. How can we reduce his anxiety and thereby increase the energy he has available for learning?

a. tell him not to worry about it . . . turn to page 13, top.
b. stop all spelling tests . . . turn to page 13, bottom.
c. give short tests on words learned each day . . . turn to page 14, top.
d. explain to his mother spelling is not that important . . . turn to page 14, bottom.

a. **You said to tell him not to worry about it.**

You must be kidding! With that mother? He knows only too well what will happen and he has cause to worry. If he thinks you are unconcerned, he will probably worry more. Turn back to page 12 and select an answer that will not compound his anxiety.

b. **You said to stop all spelling tests.**

If you could do it indefinitely it might help, but what happens when you start them again? You and he are right back in the same fix. Besides, how are you going to know whether or not your teaching is producing results? Turn back to page 12 and select an answer that will reduce tension but not eliminate the amount needed for learning.

c. **You said to give short tests on words learned each day.**

That is an excellent idea! You will accomplish two things. First, you will eliminate the compounding effect of anxiety that builds all week and hinges on one fatal performance. Daily tests are not so important (to Johnny and mother), the possibility for success is greater, and every day he has a fresh chance to make good.

Second, both teacher and children have immediate feedback on what has been accomplished so that appropriate decisions can be made to move faster or slower. Each student can experiment with different methods for learning spelling and select the one most productive for him. Also, by avoiding the Thursday night cramming and substituting daily study, you are going to achieve longer retention. Of course, you will need to have frequent reviews to make sure a word isn't learned one day and forgotten the next, but you face that problem with the weekly test anyway.

See all dividends you receive from application of sound psychological theory? Turn to page 15 for identification of another important variable.

d. **You said we should explain to his mother that spelling isn't that important.**

You must be kidding! This will confirm her worst suspicion. If you won't put pressure on Johnny for spelling, she must. You'd better reassure her that you're doing something productive. Turn back to page 12 and choose an answer that will imply that you think doing well on a spelling test is important.

We have talked about a certain amount of concern or tension increasing motivation. When tension increases to an undue degree because of excessive anxiety, anger, hostility, or compulsion, motivation decreases. The optimum point of tension varies with each individual. The anger that will make one child persist may make another withdraw. Anxiety that will stimulate one student to increased effort will cause another to stop trying. No student comes with easy-to-read calibration: in each case the teacher must make a professional decision based on sound principles and astute, sophisticated observation.

2. Feeling Tone

Feeling tone: pleasant, unpleasant, or neutral, constitutes another dimension of motivation. Remember our hypothetical case of you reclining in an easy chair? If you had a super book and you enjoyed reading, you probably would have been reading (pleasant feeling tone). If you had a professional conscience, as a result of the telephone calls you would have become motivated to read this program to avoid disgracing yourself by missing questions (unpleasant feeling tone). If you didn't enjoy reading and didn't give a hoot about the test, you just would have settled back and done nothing (neutral feeling tones).

So we arrive at our psychological generalization. Pleasant feeling tones will increase motivation to a high degree. Unpleasant feeling tones will also increase motivation, but to a lesser degree (and there may be undesirable side effects). Neutral or absence of feeling tone won't do a thing. Translated into classroom procedure, making Jimmy feel good about neat papers will motivate him. Making him unhappy about sloppy papers will also motivate him. But just "letting him be" will get you and him nowhere.

Let's supply this principle to some reluctant pupils who don't want to be bothered with the chore of learning the multiplication facts. Which procedure should be the most effective for the majority of learners?

a. giving a test and placing on the bulletin board the names of those who knew their multiplication facts . . . turn to page 16, top.
b. giving the test and keeping after school those who didn't know their multiplication facts . . . turn to page 16, bottom.
c. letting children know you are going to give a test . . . turn to page 17, top.
d. keeping your own anxiety level down by not worrying about it . . . turn to page 17, bottom.

15

a. You said you would give a test and place on the bulletin board the names of those who knew their multiplication facts.

Good for you! You will be surprised by what this will accomplish. Not all of the sinners will be brought into the fold, but the majority will respond to the pleasant feeling tone by being highly motivated to do even better the next time. You have, also, achieved the added dividend of associating pleasant feelings with multiplication (which is *really* an innovation). This could spread to all mathematics. Turn to page 18 to see what you do for those "lazy bones" who just don't care.

b. You said you would give a test and keep after school those who didn't know their multiplication facts.

You may need to. If you do, you will be creating unpleasant feeling tone and increasing motivation. However, there are the possible side-effects of disliking multiplication in particular and mathematics in general. You don't want to take a chance on this unless you have already tried pleasant feeling tones and found they won't do the job. Turn back to page 15 and choose an answer that you would try first.

c. You said you would let children know you are going to give a test.

This will raise their anxiety level all right, but how are you practicing using pleasant, unpleasant and neutral feeling tones as an aid to motivation? Turn back to page 15 and choose an answer that will involve the most effective aspect of this variable.

d. You said you would keep your own anxiety level down by not worrying about it.

That won't help anything. Our guess is that, as a teacher, there is nothing that will raise your anxiety level more than a student who is not learning. Go back to page 15 and choose an answer that will do something about it.

Pleasant feeling tone will increase motivation, but there are always a few "happy" individuals who are unaffected. To keep them from remaining in their satisfied and uninvolved state, we need to "jar" them. For those who haven't been motivated to learn their multiplication facts by pleasant feeling tone we may need to:

a. explain the importance of accuracy in multiplication . . . turn to page 19, top.
b. reassure them that by trying hard they will learn . . . turn to page 19, bottom.
c. give special assistance with the task . . . turn to page 20, top.
d. plan multiplication sessions for them while those who have already learned are enjoying activities of their own choice . . . turn to page 20, bottom.

a. **You said we should explain the importance of accuracy in multiplication.**

You'll have a hard time doing it. Think how many situations there are in a student's life when not knowing his "tables" will really make any difference to him. Turn back to page 18 and choose an action that will really make a difference.

b. **You said we should reassure them, that by trying hard they will learn.**

They probably will, but the trick is to get them to try hard. They have gotten by so far without much effort. Turn back to page 18 and choose an answer that will stimulate them to increase their effort.

c. You said you should give special assistance with the task.

Why should you if they aren't putting out effort? Of course, if you see a reason they are having trouble you should try to remove it. Still they had better learn it's their task, not yours. Turn back to page 18 and choose an answer that will bring this to their attention.

d. You said we should plan multiplication sessions for them while those who have already learned are enjoying activities of their own choice.

What could be more fair? Isn't life that way? If you finish what you have to do, the time is yours to use as you choose. When pleasant feeling tone doesn't work, by all means use unpleasant (with judgment of course). Just be sure the feeling is a logical outcome of the student's actions and the consequences are completely fair. Leaving a child in a neutral state is the worst thing you can do, because then he will learn nothing and have to suffer more severe consequences in life.

Remember that tension and unpleasant feeling tones can have undesirable side effects. They are like a sharp knife. In the hands of someone who doesn't know the danger, they can hurt. In the hands of a professional they are mighty useful.

Turn to page 21 to read about some variables that are directly related to the task and are powerful in increasing motivation.

3. Interest

We have talked about manipulating the degree of tension or concern and the kind of feeling tone in an effort to increase motivation. There are some variables, directly related to the task, that are highly responsive to our "tinkering." One of the most obvious is *interest*. We are motivated to do the things that interest us. If we, as teachers, can increase a child's interest, his motivation will increase. Knowing this, you should no longer be willing to assign dull, repetitious tasks without trying to give them some spark.

Let's go back to Sally, who was majoring in boys and ignoring her math paper. Suppose, instead of straight multiplication we give her a problem from life. It reads:

Teenagers today are usually allowed to go out two nights a week during the school year. How many dates will the average high school girl have between September and June?

In changing Sally's assignment, what variable are you trying to manipulate to increase motivation?

a. level of tension . . . turn to page 22, top.
b. nature of feeling tone . . . turn to page 22, bottom.
c. difficulty of task . . . turn to page 23, top.
d. interest . . . turn to page 23, bottom.

a. You said you were trying to manipulate level of tension.

If you mean Sally's anxiety about whether or not she can go out two nights a week when she is in high school, you may be right. This, however, will have nothing to do with increasing her motivation to do her math assignment. Turn back to page 21 and select an answer that will encourage her to solve the problem.

b. You said you were trying to manipulate the kind of feeling tone.

Whether pleasant, unpleasant, or neutral feeling tone is aroused depends on Sally's estimate of what will happen to her when she is in high school. This couldn't be less related to her desire to finish her mathematics. Turn back to page 21 and select an answer that might result in her motivation to solve the problem.

c. You said you were manipulating the difficulty of the task.

If the computation is easier or harder than the problems formerly assigned, you may be; but that was not indicated by the situation as we described it. Turn back to page 21 and select an answer that shows we are doing something specifically related to Sally.

d. You said you were manipulating the variable of "interest."

Of course you were! What could be more interesting to a young lady with her mind on boys than computing the number of dates she might have. Now mind you, we are not recommending this as a solution for young ladies who aren't interested in math, but as an example of using a student's interest as a motivating factor. For a reluctant reader, finding a book on a subject with which he is fascinated, making assignments novel and exciting, and relating abstract learning (like motivation principles) to the problems faced in everyday life are all examples of manipulating the variable of interest so that motivation is increased.

We hope you are interested in learning about other variables. Turn to the next page.

4. Success

You are usually more successful in activities that interest you; and your success in turn tends to stimulate increased interest. For this reason, degree of *success* becomes an important variable in motivation. Very few people continue to be motivated in activities where they feel they have experienced little or no success.

It is important to separate the concept of success from the idea of doing something with little or no effort. You have no feeling of success as a result of reading these words because there is little chance that they are hard for you. But, someone learning English, or even the typical seven year old, would experience a feeling of success from correctly pronouncing the words on this page.

If you are new to motivation principles, you should have a feeling of success if you select correct answers as you go through this program. On the other hand, a sophisticated learning theorist would not experience that feeling. *Degree of difficulty* is closely related to success, though it is not exactly the same. Usually if something is extremely difficult for us, we are not successful in accomplishing it. Occasionally, a herculean task is successfully accomplished and forgotten just as fast as possible. Usually motivation is optimized by a task of a moderate degree of difficulty so that by accomplishing it we experience success.

By now you are probably astute enough to relate "trying hard" with the development of optimum tension or concern and achievement of success with pleasant feeling tone.

Let's apply what we have learned so far and decide which of the following students is most highly motivated to learn at school.

a. the successful student . . . turn to page 25, top.
b. the failing student . . . turn to page 25, bottom.
c. the student whose parents hold education in high regard . . . turn to page 26, top.
d. the student who finds school work extremely easy . . . turn to page 26, bottom.

a. **You said the successful student was the most highly motivated to learn.**

That's right! He is experiencing success so he is probably interested and as a result glows with pleasant feeling tone. We are assuming that he had to work to earn his success, so he is operating under the moderate tension which should increase his motivation. It makes us stop to think about the complaint that "unsuccessful students just aren't motivated" doesn't it?

The successful student is reaping the benefit of one other important variable. Turn to page 27 to see what it is.

b. **You said the failing student was the most highly motivated.**

People think he should be, but after reading this program you know better. Lack of success generates unpleasant feeling tone. This, together with the degree of tension generated by failing, will usually result in a "don't care" attitude which changes the feeling tone to neutral. Not trying for a while will result in a child's getting behind so that the work really is too difficult and there is no chance of success. It is obvious we are listing all the factors that lead to decreased motivation, so turn back to page 24 and select a student who has had the opposite experience.

c. **You said the student whose parents hold education in high regard, is most highly motivated.**

The two factors are related all right, but a student's motivation is dependent on what parents do about their feelings. Over-demanding parents can produce an inert, unmotivated, or even a resistant student. If the parents' feelings are contributing to the child's motivation, turn back to page 24 and find a better description of that child.

d. **You said the student who finds school work extremely easy is the most highly motivated.**

What does he have to be motivated about? There is nothing interesting about a task that can be accomplished with little or no effort. He probably hasn't even had to try hard enough to experience the feeling of success. He is usually bored. There isn't enough feeling tone or tension to generate any steam. Turn back to page 24 and select a student whose motivation will propel him.

5. Knowledge of Results

"Knowledge of results" is the psychological term for the feedback that answers the question, "How am I doing?" The answer to that question has a powerful influence on our state of motivation. Picture yourself trying to hit a target but never knowing whether or not you had. Or think of trying to lose weight without a scale or tape measure or even a tight belt to give you "knowledge of results."

The more specific feedback we get, the more we become motivated to improve our performance. We react differently to "You didn't hit the target" and to "Your shot was much too high and a little bit to the left of center."

Giving students highly specific knowledge of results usually yields increased motivation. Using this generalization, which statement would result in increased motivation to do a better social studies outline?

a. "You made an A on your outline.". . . turn to page 28, top.
b. "You did an excellent job on your general points, but you need to include more supporting evidence on page 2, 5, and 7.". . . turn to page 28, bottom.
c. "You did the best outline in the room.". . . turn to page 29, top.
d. "You did not include enough detail.". . . turn to page 29, bottom.

a. **You said, "You made an 'A' on your last outline."**

You have given the student the general information that he has met expectations well, but now what is he to do? He vaguely knows he should do the same thing, but what is it? He may have received an "A" for a fair outline because all the rest of the class still didn't understand outlining. He may have received an "A" for a truly superb job of distilling content; if so, he should know it. Grades are so general they are at the low end of the "knowledge of results" continuum.

Turn back to page 27 and choose an answer that will be at the "specific knowledge of results" end.

b. **You said, "You did an excellent job on your general points but need to include more supporting evidence on pages 2, 5, and 7."**

You did an excellent job on giving him knowledge of results and you *did* include the evidence to support your evaluation. Consequently, the student knows what is satisfactory and what he needs to work on. As a result, his motivation should increase and his product be improved.

Turn to page 30 for the last variable we can manipulate to increase motivation.

c. You said, "You did the best outline in the room."

This may be good or bad depending on which room he is in. Besides, if you are satisfied with his performance, he is not motivated to change or improve it. Granted the pleasant feeling tone that goes with success is beneficial; a little tension is needed to generate the energy to improve performance. Knowledge of results is then needed to direct that energy. Turn back to page 27 and choose an answer that will give more information.

d. You said, "You did not include enough detail."

You are giving him *some* knowledge of results. He now knows the thing about his performance he needs to change, but he doesn't know that the quality of the rest of his performance was good. He may even change the part he was doing well. Turn back to page 27 and select the answer that will give him the most specific information.

6. Intrinsic-Extrinsic Motivation

We have discussed tension, feeling tone, success, difficulty of task, interest and knowledge of results. Now we come to the last variable, the *relationship of the reward or goal to the activity necessary to secure it*. Reading a book (activity) because you enjoy reading (reward or goal) is an example of high relationship of the activity to the goal. Doing your reading homework (activity) to get out of doing the dishes (goal) is an example of little relationship of the activity to the goal. This is the essence of the difference between intrinsic and extrinsic motivation.

Intrinsic motivation is not saintly and extrinsic motivation sinful. Both are effective, but because of the direct relationship between activity and goal, an intrinsically motivated activity will always be rewarded. You can always secure the reward of enjoyment of reading by the activity of reading so your motivation to read is constantly compounded. Activity that is extrinsically motivated secures the goal in some circumstances, but not in others. Reading your homework will get the dishes done if mother thinks you should study, but it won't do a thing about the dishes if you are in your own apartment. Consequently, the power of extrinsic motivation is controlled by the environmental circumstances and changes with the environment.

We are all familiar with the teacher who has ironclad discipline when she is in the room and chaos when she is out. This is a typical example of extrinsic motivation. The activity (good behavior) produces the reward (keeping the teacher happy) as long as you have the same teacher. If you change teachers, you have to rediscover what will keep the new one happy. Contrast this situation with the class that behaves because the students enjoy an orderly, productive classroom. Here the activity should always secure the goal.

Intrinsic motivation has the advantage that, once you discover the activity necessary to the goal, it remains constant. With extrinsic motivation you have to assess the environment anew each time in order to determine the activity to achieve the goal.

Intrinsic and extrinsic are on opposite ends of a continuum with most examples of motivation being not completely one nor the other. The following examples are often used as being intrinsically motivated. Select the one that demonstrates the greatest intrinsic motivation.

a. doing a math assignment because you enjoy math ... turn to page 32, top.
b. subtracting what you spent from what you earned to find out how much you have left ... turn to page 32, bottom.
c. working hard in math to get a good grade ... turn to page 33, top.
d. working for an "A" in math so you can get into college ... turn to page 33, bottom.

a. **You said doing a math assignment because you enjoy math showed the greatest intrinsic motivation.**

It is more intrinsic than extrinsic, but there are other activities that could lead to the goal. Making up your own problems, finding new ways to solve problems and talking about math to someone else who is interested could all be more directly related to your goal of enjoyment of math. If the assignment is far too hard or boringly easy, your doing it won't bring you enjoyment at all.

Turn back to page 31 and choose an answer where the activity will always secure the goal.

b. **You said subtracting what you spent from what you earned to find out how much you have left showed the greatest intrinsic motivation.**

Right you are! That activity will always produce the goal. This is why in school we need to try to relate learning to the way it will be used all through life. Incidentally, this is one reason we have so much trouble teaching spelling. Our goal is to communicate in writing. The activity selected to achieve that goal is tiresome lists or oral spelling. "Thay R naught reely related ar thay?" Now turn to page 34.

c. You said working hard in math to get a good grade showed the greatest intrinsic motivation.

Not necessarily. Flattering the teacher, doing neat papers, being the son of a mayor, or joining actively in classroom discussions could be more effective. Besides, working like a dog is to no avail if you are in a math class that is far beyond your ability. Turn back to page 31 and select an answer that is more related to the goal.

d. You said working for an "A" in math so you can get in college showed the greatest intrinsic motivation.

Not necessarily. An "F" in French may ruin your chance of achieving the goal. Some colleges use a comprehensive exam where your "A" will do you no good unless you have remembered what you learned. Turn back to page 31 and select an answer where the activity is more directly related to the goal.

The following types of examples are often cited when extrinsic motivation is discussed. Select the one that demonstrates the greatest extrinsic motivation.

a. working because you get a dollar for each "A" . . . turn to page 35, top.
b. doing the dishes because you can't play ball unless they are done . . . turn to page 35, bottom.
c. pushing a colored button in a psychology laboratory to secure a gum drop . . . turn to page 36, top.
d. reading this program because you have to . . . turn to page 36, bottom.

a. **You said working because you get a dollar for each "A" demonstrated the greatest extrinsic motivation.**

It's extrinsic all right, because getting an "A" won't help if the dollar has been offered for washing the car. The activity and goal have some relationship, however, for engaging in the activity desired by the person who has the money in order to get the money is an important relationship. It hasn't been discovered by the people who feel they ought to be paid for doing as they choose.

Turn back to page 34 and select an answer where the activity and the reward have less relationship.

b. **You said "doing the dishes" because you can't play ball until they are done demonstrates the greatest extrinsic motivation.**

It is extrinsic all right, because doing the dishes is not going to help if mother thinks the floor needs sweeping before you can get out. The activity and goal have some relationship, however, for doing what you have to do in order to be free to do what you would like to do is an important relationship. It hasn't been discovered by the people who don't accept their responsibilities.

Turn back to page 34 and select an answer where the activity and the reward have less relationship.

c. You said pushing a colored button in a psychology lab to secure a gum drop demonstrates the greatest extrinsic motivation.

You are absolutely right! It would be hard to find anything with less relationship between activity and reward. That is why it has been selected for an experimental task. You can't bring previous generalizations about activity-reward relationships to contaminate the controlled conditions. Hopefully we never do anything so unrelated in a classroom. But rote memorization of material about which the student has no understanding in order to secure a grade is a close approximation to complete extrinsic motivation.

We hope the activity of turning to the next page is related to a goal of learning more about motivation.

d. You said reading this program because you have to, demonstrates the greatest extrinsic motivation.

It is extrinsic all right, because reading this program won't help if the thing you "have to do" is something else. The activity and the goal have some relationship however; doing what you have to do achieves the reward of getting it done and over with. It is obvious this relationship has not been discovered by our reluctant students who expend more energy avoiding the task than it would take to accomplish it.

Turn back to page 34 and select an answer where the activity and reward have even less relationship.

By now you have probably discovered that when the activity itself is rewarding (enjoying reading or swimming) we have a situation where motivation is intrinsic, i.e., the activity will always achieve the goal and motivation compounds. Playing ball because you enjoy playing ball will always achieve the goal. Playing to achieve the goal of beating the other team is always problematical.

Let's summarize what we have read: 1. Motivation implies the student is no longer in passive equilibrium, but as a result of some unresolved need or desire is activated to change his behavior in order to achieve some goal. Wanting or needing that goal has caused the disequilibrium. 2. We as teachers can manipulate variables in the environment that are related to:

a. *Tension or concern.* This is a facilitating factor providing it exists to a moderate degree. Too much tension may divert the learner's energy into dealing with the tension rather than the learning task.
b. *Feeling tone.* A moderate amount of pleasant or unpleasant tone will increase motivation, while excessive amounts produce debilitating tension. Absence of feeling tone, or neutral feeling tones, tend to decrease motivation.
c. *Interest.* The more interest we can generate, the greater the learning dividends.
d. *Success.* Unsuccessful effort or tasks that are too difficult depress motivation. Success and the right degree of difficulty increase motivation.
e. *Knowledge of results.* The more specific the feedback on performance, the more motivation should increase.
f. *Relation of activity to reward.* When the activity itself is rewarding, it produces a situation where motivation is intrinsic, the activity will always achieve the goal, and motivation compounds. Extrinsic motivation is dependent on and changes with the specific environmental situation.

It is important that we remember that no one of the above conditions is more potent than the others. We must also realize that different learners respond to manipulation of different variables. No one of these variables exists in complete independence of the others. All are interrelated. We have separated them for the purpose of learning about them, but we work with many of them at one time concentrating on those that are most responsive to our manipulation.

The importance of each variable varies with the individual and the situation. This is reassuring to us as teachers, for when one condition is beyond our control we do not need to give up but can manipulate one of the others.

We hope that your reading this program developed a state of moderate tension, which has been accompanied by pleasant feeling tone as a result of receiving knowledge of your success in choosing correct answers. If we have generated interest in applying your knowledge of motivation principles, you will find the activity itself is rewarding as your students respond favorably. You will become intrinsically motivated to apply sound psychological principles to solve learning problems, for there couldn't be a more direct relationship of activity to goal!

MOTIVATION THEORY
SELF-TEST

If you wish to further increase your motivation, take this test so the knowledge of results of how much you have learned will increase your motivation.

1. A teacher who wished to increase the accuracy of students' computation should find most effective:
   a. telling each child how many problems he has done correctly
   b. telling each child how many problems he has done incorrectly
   c. children correcting each other's papers
   d. children correcting their own papers
   e. giving letter grades to each paper

2. By initiating a social studies unit with an arranged environment, the teacher is trying to increase motivation to learn by:
   a. meaningfulness
   b. manipulation
   c. success
   d. interest
   e. feeling tone

3. Modern education states that one of the most important outcomes of schooling is the development of a zest for learning. This objective is based on the motivational influence of:
   a. feeling tone
   b. success
   c. knowledge of results
   d. intrinsic motivation
   e. tension

4. Ralph has great difficulty in handwriting and never works to improve it. Poor motivation would probably result from his lack of:
   a. interest
   b. knowledge of results
   c. feeling tone
   d. activity related to goal
   e. success

5. Paul avoids all physical education because he is afraid of being hit by a ball. He does not throw or catch well. What will probably be the most effective technique to increase his motivation?
   a. assure him that playing ball is fun
   b. get the other children to help him
   c. let him know the importance of participation in games
   d. teach him to throw and catch
   e. be sure he is successful in other parts of the day

6. You feel it is important that children learn how to prepare a report on a country that deals with the history, geography, government, and customs, but they seem unmotivated. You begin by having them work on the section on geography with much help from you. What variable are you manipulating?
   a. knowledge of results
   b. success
   c. interest
   d. feeling tone
   e. level of difficulty

7. Bill is poorly coordinated so the teacher skates with him as his partner when the class is rollerskating. Bill begins to enjoy the physical sensations of skating. His motivation to learn to skate will probably increase most as a result of:
   a. reduction of his anxiety
   b. attention by the teacher
   c. more chance of success
   d. the reward's relation to the activity
   e. skating is becoming easier

8. When you call on two strong students in succession for the first responses in a new drill, then two average students, and lastly, a weak student, you are manipulating the motivational variable of:
   a. success
   b. feeling tone
   c. tension
   d. interest
   e. level of difficulty

9. When you dismiss class members individually (at the time for going home) by requiring each to give the correct answer to a multiplication fact, you are manipulating the motivational variable of:
   a. success
   b. knowledge of results
   c. tension
   d. interest
   e. level of difficulty

10. The teacher decides to tally on the board the number of times the class can follow instructions without unnecessary questions as well as the number of times unnecessary questions are asked. To increase the motivation to listen carefully, she is manipulating the variable of:
    a. success
    b. interest
    c. feeling tone
    d. knowledge of results
    e. intrinsic motivation

11. Choose the statement that describes the most *extrinsic* motivation.
    a. child is building a skate board so he can ride with other children
    b. child is computing how much his father owes him
    c. child is studying hard to get straight "A's"
    d. child is swimming on a hot day
    e. child is making cookies for a party

12. It is important that unmotivated children keep records of their progress so they are influenced by:
    a. more success
    b. more interest
    c. relation of goal to activity
    d. feeling tone
    e. knowledge of results

13. Although Ralph hates spelling, his teacher sees that he practices until he can get 100 on the test. She had probably made the decision that an important motivational factor for him is:
    a. success
    b. feeling tone
    c. knowledge of results
    d. activity related to goal
    e. tension

14. Which child will have the most productive motivation to learn?
    a. a child unconcerned about the learning
    b. a child a little concerned about the learning
    c. a child moderately concerned about the learning
    d. a child much concerned about the learning
    e. a child greatly concerned about the learning

15. The teacher wishes the intrinsic motivation of reading to increase. Which of the following should she choose?
    a. a chart where each child records the number of books he reads
    b. much recreational reading
    c. many easy books
    d. asking parents to encourage reading at home
    e. giving special recognition to good readers

Correct answers.

1 – d	6 – e	11 – c
2 – d	7 – d	12 – e
3 – d	8 – e	13 – a
4 – e	9 – c	14 – c
5 – d	10 – d	15 – b

If you have 10 or more correct –

The pleasant feeling tones of your success should motivate you to use your knowledge of motivation theory in the classroom.

If you have 5 to 9 correct –

The specific knowledge of results of which questions you missed should motivate you (we hope) to review parts of this book.

If you have less than 5 correct –

Our failure to write a better program has resulted in unpleasant feeling tones for you and us. We hope that will motivate you to write and tell us what is wrong with this book.